PROPOSALS & ENGAGEMENTS

A Guide to Happy Beginnings

JO PACKHAM

A Sterling/Chapelle Book

Sterling Publishing Co., Inc. New York

Jo Packham
Author

Cherie Hanson
Editor/Designer

Margaret Shields Marti
Executive Editor

Library of Congress Cataloging-in-Publication Data

Packham, Jo.
    Wedding proposals & engagements : a guide to happy beginnings /
by Jo Packham.
        p.   cm.
    "A Sterling/Chapelle book."
    Includes index.
    ISBN 0-8069-8835-5
    1. Weddings—United States—Planning.   I. Title.   II. Title: Wedding
proposals and engagements.
HQ745.P354 1993
395'.22—dc20   93-21518
                                                                 CIP

10 9 8 7 6 5 4 3 2 1

A Sterling/Chapelle Book

Published by Sterling Publishing Company, Inc.
387 Park Avenue South, New York, N.Y. 10016
© 1993 by Chapelle Ltd.
Distributed in Canada by Sterling Publishing
$^{c}/_{o}$ Canadian Manda Group, P.O. Box 920, Station U
Toronto, Ontario, Canada M8Z 5P9
Distributed in Great Britain and Europe by Cassell PLC
Villiers House, 41/47 Strand, London WC2N 5JE, England
Distributed in Australia by Capricorn Link Ltd.
P.O. Box 665, Lane Cove, NSW 2066
Manufactured in the United States of America

Sterling ISBN 0-8069-8835-5

I've often wished to have a friend
With whom my choicest hours to spend,
To whom I safely may impart
Each wish and weakness of my heart.
Who would in every sorrow cheer,
And mingle with my grief a tear,
And to secure that bliss for life,
I'd like that friend to be my wife.

Unknown

Contents

Introduction

Legends tell that, in the earliest days, when a man was seeking a wife, he simply hunted her, captured her and dragged her away to live with him in his home. His selection was not motivated because of his love for her or because she was beautiful or desirable. He made his decision based upon her ability to work and her potential to breed new workers. Gradually, marriage by capture became a game of courtship which had a myriad of rules, depending upon the customs of the time and the location. The games of courtship were sometimes interceded by arranged marriages dictated by a family's needs, for reasons of politics or economic transfer. For many generations and in many locations, marriage was a practical merger of labor and property between two families or two countries, not an expression of love and romance between a man and a woman. For a time, marriage also became an avenue of proving a man's status and wealth–the more wives he had, the more important he became. This ancient philosophy, which began with King Solomon who had 700 wives, continues in certain countries even today.

For most of us in our society, however, a new bride is chosen because of a word called "love." The dictionary tells us love is "a deep and tender feeling of affection for or attachment or devotion to a person or persons." The definition is correct but seems to miss the essence of "this thing called 'love'," yet few have been able to describe it any better.

Henry Van Dyke stated,
"There are as many kinds of love as many kinds of light,
And every kind of love makes a glory in the night.
There is love that stirs the heart, and love that gives it rest,
But the love that leads life upwards is the noblest and the best."

And the German philosopher Friedrich Wilhelm Nietzsche said,
"Love is the state in which man sees things most widely different from what they are."

Your Engagement

For the groom:

Falling in love is, indeed, the most exciting and unpredictable part of any relationship. It often takes much longer than our dreams or expectations had thought it would. According to one study, thirty percent of the men polled could not say for sure whether or not they were in love until after the twentieth date, while forty-three percent of the women felt the same way. Why are women, and some men, so afraid of falling in love? Because it inevitably means change and most of us are afraid of change.

Once you have decided, however, that you really are in love, that you will overcome your fears of change and the unknown, and that this is definitely the girl of your dreams, then it is probably time to propose. In the era following arranged marriages when traces of the practice still remained, you would ask the bride's father for her hand in marriage. With today's social rules and traditions, however, you may ask the girl of your dreams to become your wife in the way that is best suited to you. It can be done traditionally during a quiet evening at home, by getting down on bended knee, presenting the ring to her, and asking her to become your wife; it can be handled in a most romantic manner at a restaurant by having the waiter deliver dessert with "Will you marry me?" written on top; or it can be made with an extravagant flair by having a skywriter scrawl your proposal across the sky.

"How should I ask her?" you say. "I want her to be surprised and to always remember the moment" you may be constantly thinking. Have you considered tucking your proposal inside a fortune cookie and having the waiter deliver it with your Chinese take-out dinner; or placing an ad in the newspaper (if you are certain she reads the newspaper)? You could send the proposal by means of a singing telegram or, if money is no object, you could rent a billboard and have the proposal painted in five-foot letters. Or you could simply kiss her quietly and whisper your proposal in her ear in front of the fire on a snowy winter night.

Regardless of how you choose to propose, it will be a fairy-tale moment for your bride-to-be. It will be the magic question that causes the fantasy to become reality and the occasion that holds the hope that promises will be kept. Now, with the uttering of four small words, the transformation from being simply a woman in love into the bride of her dreams begins to take place.

The Ring

For the groom:

Why engagement rings? Why wedding rings? The engagement ring, or betrothal ring, dates back to the days of marriage by purchase. Before the introduction of coinage, gold rings were circulated as currency and a man would give his bride a gold ring as both a partial payment and as a symbol of his honorable intentions and trust–but very rarely as a display of his love. During the Elizabethan period, the "gimmal" ring or "interlocking set of rings with three parts" was most popular. At betrothal and during the period of the engagement, the bride, the groom, and their witness each wore one of the rings until the wedding day when the three pieces were reunited as a single ring for the bride. Later came the "regard" ring, which often spelled out a message of love, both literally and figuratively, with precious stones such as diamonds, emeralds, or rubies. The suitor might spell out "sweetheart" or "I love you" in precious gems and then give the ring to the lady of his dreams. In medieval Italy, the diamond was introduced into the engagement ring because of its hardness, which was chosen to represent enduring love–thus, the phrase "diamonds are forever." Today the diamond is the most popular engagement stone and is a sign of both wealth and unending devotion.

The circular shape of the engagement and wedding rings represents love that knows no beginning and has no end. Primitive brides wore wedding bands made of rush or hemp and replaced them every year, while early Romans chose iron that was more durable to represent the permanent unending nature of their marriage. The wedding band is worn on the left hand due to ancient peoples belief that the vein in the third finger of the left hand ran directly to the heart. Bridegrooms during Medieval times placed the ring on three of the bride's fingers in turn to symbolize the Trinity–the Father, the Son, and the Holy Spirit. In several cultures, the ring has remained on the left hand; however, in many European countries, the ring is now worn on the right hand. Greek women wear their ring on their left hand while engaged, changing it to the right hand when they are married. Jewish brides have the ring placed on the third finger of the right hand during the ceremony and then often-times change it to the left hand after the ceremony.

Selecting the Perfect Ring

After deciding that, yes, you should indeed get married, your first decision will be what kind of ring to give. Will it be an engagement ring or a single gold wedding band to be presented during the ceremony? Will it be new or will it be a family heirloom? Do you know which your bride prefers? Not all brides really want an engagement ring; some prefer the look of a simple gold band. Other brides, who definitely want an engagement ring, prefer that the engagement ring and the wedding band be a set intended to be worn together, while some may prefer to wear the two separately. Women who work with their hands may wear only their wedding band from one day to the next, saving their engagement ring for special occasions. Whether you decide to give an engagement ring or just a band, it is a very romantic idea to have the band engraved with a personal thought or both of your initials and the wedding date. This is definitely the one time in your life when you will want to be as sentimental as you possibly can!

Whatever you finally decide, it would be a wise decision to discuss the subject of rings openly and honestly with your bride, either before you present the ring to her or after, if you are planning a surprise. The possibility exists for more than one misunderstanding to occur, any of which can last a lifetime if the situation is not discussed very early on. For example, many grooms really do not want to wear a wedding band and yet it is very important to their bride that they have one. To avoid any hurt feelings that you are still discussing on your fiftieth wedding anniversary, you need to come to an understanding that you both agree to and sincerely feel good about from the beginning!

Deciding on when to give your bride-to-be her ring will determine when you should begin shopping for and finally purchase the set. Are you going to give her an engagement ring or only a wedding band? Do you want her to help select the ring–after all, she is the one who is going to be wearing it for the rest of her life–or do you want to surprise her with it? Even if you want the proposal and the presentation of the ring to be a surprise, there are a number of ways to find out what kind of ring your intended would like and what size she wears.

You can take her to several jewelry stores on the pretense of buying a ring for your mother for a gift and listen to what she says as she is helping you decide what to buy. Does she like diamonds or a more unusual stone? Does she like simple solitary settings or ones that have a multitude of smaller stones? Does she prefer gold or silver? Have her try on a ring of your mother's to see if they wear the same size or borrow one of hers without her knowing and get it sized. If you are very careful, you can find out everything you need to know without her suspecting. Or, if you have talked about marriage, and she knows that marriage to you is in her future, then you might arrange the following: The two of you enjoy a very romantic dinner in a tiny, quiet restaurant and then late, when all of the stores are closed, you could go window shopping. She could show you the ring she likes and hopes someday to wear. If you ask lots of questions and listen carefully, you can learn more about one another in these quiet moments than you might have realized. Sharing these kinds of activities and dreams can bring the two of you closer and–trust me–an activity such as this one will not spoil the surprise. It will only add to the memories.

Engagement and wedding rings can be found in a variety of locations. They are sold in jewelry store chains, department stores with jewelry departments, independent jewelry stores, and self-proclaimed jewelry wholesalers. You, or both you and your bride, will want to visit several of the choices to compare styles, quality of gems and workmanship and price. Be careful and only look for reputable companies. Ask friends for recommendations and ask the jeweler if he/she is a member of the American Gem Society, an organization that sets high ethical standards and provides advanced education for jewelers and their employees.

The most common settings for engagement and wedding rings are gold, white gold and silver, all of which have a platinum head to hold the stone or stones in place. Most rings you will see in stores are a combination of gold and a second metal which gives the ring its strength. Pure gold is twenty-four-karat gold and would be too soft for jewelry. Twelve-karat is half gold and half another metal. That other metal determines both the strength and the color of the ring. Eighteen-karat white gold is 75 percent gold and, probably, 25 percent platinum; eighteen-karat yellow gold is 75 percent gold, 9.5 percent silver, and 15.5 percent copper. The more copper and less silver produces a rose-colored gold.

Traditionally, brides selected engagement rings with diamonds, a solitaire setting in yellow gold being the most popular. Contemporary brides, however, are selecting a myriad of stones and settings for their wedding rings. They may choose their birthstone surrounding a single diamond or have a rainbow of stones that encircle the entire band. Whatever stone or setting your bride-to-be wants the most is the one you should select because the only "right" or "wrong" is whether or not she likes it.

If your bride decides for sentimental reasons that she wants her birthstone in her engagement ring, they are as follows:

```
January. . . . . . . . . . . . . . . . . . . . . Garnet
February. . . . . . . . . . . . . . . . . .Amethyst
March . . . . . . . Aquamarine or Bloodstone
April . . . . . . . . . . . . . . . . . . . . .Diamond
May . . . . . . . . . . . . . . . . . . . . . .Emerald
June . . . . . . . . . . . . . . . . . . . . . . . .Pearl
July . . . . . . . . . . . . . . . . . . . . . . . .Ruby
August. . . . . . . . .Sardonyx or Carnelian
September. . . . . . . . . . . . . . . . Sapphire
October. . . . . . . . . .Opal or Moonstone
November. . . . . . . . . . . . . . . . . . . Topaz
December. . . Turquoise or Lapis Lazuli
```

Gems, like flowers, have folklore attached to them. Every stone has some "wisdom" to share with the recipient.

Amethyst: According to biblical lore, the amethyst is equal to perfection. The Roman women wore this gem as a symbol of faithfulness and sincerity because they believed it would ensure a husband's love.

Aquamarine: Folklore has it that the person who wears this stone is said to be able to read another's thoughts. It is also believed to make the wearer intelligent and courageous.

Diamond: This stone is considered a symbol of matrimonial happiness and is believed to protect the wearer from evil spirits. The diamond is also an emblem of innocence. Storytellers say that if a husband wants to know whether his bride has been faithful, he should hold the diamond over her head while she sleeps. If she turns toward him, she is faithful and true but, if she turns away, she has had another lover.

Emerald: This gem is believed to hold the key to domestic bliss and success in love.

Garnet: Legend says that if you want someone to love you, you should give him/her a garnet; it is the stone that stands for eternal, true friendship.

Ruby: The ruby is the "sun's own gem" and is said to house a warm and endless flame. Because it is considered a sign of love, legends say that the ruby engagement ring will change color and darken if the course of true love is not running smoothly. If everything is perfect, it will be a lighter shade of red. It is also believed that it will ward off evil spirits and bad dreams, thus protecting the wearer.

Sapphire: As a birthstone, this gem stands for truth and faithfulness and, according to legend, it brings the wearer good health and good fortune.

About Diamonds & Precious Stones

If you decide that you are more traditional than you had realized and you choose to buy your bride-to-be a diamond, then understanding what the diamond industry calls the four C's– color, clarity, cut, and carat weight–will help you know what you are looking for. It could, also, prevent your making an unwise purchase from an unscrupulous jeweler.

The **color** of diamonds can vary greatly even if, at first glance, all diamonds appear colorless. The Gemological Institute of America grades color in diamonds with letters, starting with D, which are the rarest with a hint of blue coloring and are the clearest, going down to Z, which have overtones of yellow. Most diamonds that are purchased are in the H range, which are clear to the naked eye and a colorless white.

When selecting colored gemstones, they should be intense in color, radiant and clear without reaching the point that it appears you can see through them. Aquamarines should be very, very blue; emeralds should be a rich, lush green; rubies should look pinkish-red; and sapphires should be cornflower blue.

The **clarity** of a diamond, which is its degree of freedom from internal flaws, is the first thing to look for in a stone. As diamonds form, not all of the carbon is crystallized, leaving some minute particles to remain black, which, when found in a stone, are referred to as inclusions. Most of these flaws are invisible to the eye and can be detected only by the use of a jeweler's microscope. A stone with a few inclusions at the edge, near the girdle, where the bezel may hide them, will be more valuable than a diamond with the same number of inclusions in the table, or flat top of the gem, where they are more visible.

The **cut** of a stone refers to the arrangement of the facets or the polished flat planes of the stone and is one of the easiest ways to appraise the value of the stone. Fine stones with good cuts are fairly easy to detect because they are cut by master gem cutters, not by beginning stone cutters. Stones are cut into one of several shapes with the round, or solitaire, being the most popular, due to the fact that such a brilliant cut reflects the light so well. They can also be cut into a marquise (pointed at both ends), an oval, a pear, or an emerald cut (square or rectangular). The better the cut, the more the stone reflects light and the more it will sparkle. When selecting a diamond, there are several points in a good cut that your jeweler should discuss with and be able to point out to you.

If you are selecting a diamond engagement ring, the **carat** of the stone is the unit of weight used to measure the diamond. There are 100 points to a carat, and a stone weighing less than a carat may be referred to by its points, such as 23 points or .23 carats. You will often hear diamonds referred to in terms of fractions, such as ½ or ¼ carat, which can be misleading. A quarter-carat diamond can be anywhere from 23 to 28 points, so it is important to find out the actual weight so you know exactly what you are purchasing.

Actual terms differ according to the jeweler, but color, clarity, and the cut of precious stones are rated. One set of classifications follows:

Royal - exceptional color, clarity, and cut. These stones are rare with one in hundreds meeting this classification.

Classic - excellent color, clarity, and cut with a slightly lesser degree than royal. This is a very beautiful stone.

Regal - good color, clarity, and cut but does not meet the very high standards of the two higher classifications. This, however, will probably be the best value for couples who wish to have a large stone at a reasonable price.

Radiant - fair color, clarity, and cut are evident in this stone, which is the least expensive if you want a large diamond but cannot afford any of the three higher qualities.

Buying the Ring

When you seriously begin shopping for an engagement ring, whether it be a diamond or other precious stone, you should remember the following:

1. Set a budget for the ring and do not increase it after you have begun looking. It is very easy to "find the perfect ring" and talk yourself into spending considerably more than you can afford. Financial experts will advise that you not spend more than three weeks' salary, or 6 percent of your income, on the engagement ring. Even though it is true you want everything to be perfect and you want your bride-to-be to have the ring of her dreams, you do not want to have it become a financial burden when there are so many other expenditures, both expected and unexpected, that will occur in relation to the wedding.

2. Make certain the jeweler is reputable, which can be determined in part by how much information he is willing to give you and the amount of time he is willing to spend with you. Ask if he custom-makes rings, if he casts his own gold or sets his own precious stones. Is he a certified gemologist? Make certain he shows you several rings and that you place them side-by-side for comparison.

Only a disreputable jeweler will show you one ring at a time and pressure you to purchase it on the spot by offering you a "one-time discount" if you buy today.

3. Take a note pad and pencil and take notes on all of the rings that you see and like. If you see several rings you like in two or three stores, it becomes very difficult to remember the facts about each one after you leave the store.

4. Never buy the ring the same day. Go home, think about it, and go back three or four days later to make certain you like it as much the second time.

5. Before making the final purchase of the stone, get an outside appraisal. This should be done as a condition of the sale. Take the stone to an independent, qualified appraiser and have him give you a written document that ensures the quality of the stone and the setting.

6. Ask the jeweler about warranties and guarantees. If you find a discrepancy in the appraiser's grading of the stone with what the jeweler told you, will all of your money be refunded? If you buy the ring and your bride would rather have something else, will the jeweler exchange or refund your money so she may select the ring she wants? Is

there an unconditional, money-back guarantee if the stone is returned within a certain number of days?

7. Ask the jeweler about his repair policies. Sizing, cleaning, and tightening of the stone should be done free of charge for the first six months or year. How much does he charge after that time?

8. Be sure your receipt describes the ring and setting in detail, including the weight, shape, and color so that you may use it for insurance purposes. Some insurance companies, however, will require a written document from the jeweler; the receipt alone may not be adequate proof.

9. Make certain to check with your insurance company in regard to jewelry. The rings can be insured on your basic homeowner's policy, but make certain they are listed separately and that you understand completely what they are insured against, be it theft and/or loss. Always read the fine print; insurance companies often include clauses such as "the ring is only insured if the entire ring is lost, not if only the stone is lost." Precious stones increase in value over the years, so you will need to have the rings reappraised about every five years and adjust your insurance coverage accordingly.

For the bride:

The Groom's Engagement Ring

Do you want to give the groom an engagement ring? Does he want one? They are becoming more and more popular in certain parts of the country. Does he want a wedding band? Will it match your band or be different? Will it be of a more traditional nature, such as a solid gold band, or will it be more contemporary and contain a variety of precious stones or distinct engravings. Will you surprise him with it or will he help you pick it out?

You will want to consider the same options as discussed for the groom and follow the same guidelines when shopping for his wedding ring.

The violet loves a sunny bank,
The cowslip loves the lea;
The scarlet creeper loves the elm,
But I love, – thee! . . .

The Oriole weds his mottled mate,
The lily weds the bee;
Heaven's marriage ring is round the earth,
Let mine bind thee?

Announcing Your Engagement

For the bride:

Regardless of how or when it happens, becoming engaged stirs a whirlwind of emotions that bring daydreams into the realm of reality and sends you spinning into a future filled with hopes and romantic expectations. Parties and plans and the delightful feeling of being the bride are what you have to look forward to once the news is out that you are going to be married.

Becoming engaged is the first link in this new and exciting chain of events and announcing the engagement is link number two. Announcing your engagement can be as much fun for everyone involved as it was for the two of you to become engaged. You and your fiancé will want to tell both sets of parents of the good news before anyone else. Traditionally, the two of you go to your parents first, announce the engagement and ask for their blessing. Instead of simply walking in the door and making your announcement, you may invite them to dinner and for dessert serve a cake with "We're engaged" written on it. Although it may seem somewhat archaic, it is still a very nice and much appreciated gesture for the groom to explain his intentions and plans to your parents. After informing your parents of your recent engagement, you will want to personally visit the groom's parents and make the same announcement. Unless circumstances make it impossible to do otherwise, do not make such an announcement over the phone or in a letter. If one or both parents live a great distance from you, plan a nice weekend when the two of you can visit and tell them of your plans.

If one or both of you has been married before and has children, you will want to tell them of the engagement first. This is probably best handled on a one-to-one basis without your intended present. This allows each child the opportunity to openly express his or her feelings, which will be many and varied. Before you make any announcement to either your children or the groom's, the two of you should discuss how the children will be involved in the wedding festivities themselves. Letting them know from the very first minute that they are very important in your new relationship and that they will play a major role in the upcoming wedding festivities will help them feel important, wanted, and needed. If, however, they seem reluctant to participate in the wedding plans, do not press the issue. Time and the coming events may change their minds naturally.

After the announcement has been made and the children have had a sufficient amount of time to adjust to this new set of circumstances, then a meeting should be planned with everyone—you, the children, and your fiancé. You should inform your ex-spouse of your new plans personally and immediately after the children and both sets of parents. This may or may not be a good time to discuss the changes your upcoming marriage will cause for all of you. If your relationship is an amicable one, your ex-partner can help alleviate some of the children's fears. If your relationship is less than friendly, then you will have to deal with the announcement and your future plans in a manner that you feel is best for everyone involved.

After you have informed both sets of parents, you will want to tell close family and friends of your good news. Grandmothers, in particular, like to be among the first to hear! The announcement can be made by means of a telephone call or a handwritten note, for friends and family who live too far for you to travel to tell them the news in person. Your announcement might be a handwritten note on the inside of a card that has a separate, recent picture of you and your fiancé or pictures taken when you were much, much younger. The recipients will be delighted at your thoughtfulness and creativity.

Newspaper Announcements

At this point, you may choose to announce your engagement officially by placing a notice in the newspaper. After you have decided on a wedding date, this can be done as soon as possible. It can coincide with an engagement party, or the announcement can appear anywhere from one month to one year before the wedding. Because so many of today's families are so mobile, you may choose to have the announcement appear in several different cities' papers. It should appear in the papers in the town in which both you and your fiancé reside, both of your hometowns (if different from your current residence and if you have not been gone for too long), and where both sets of parents reside.

Every newspaper has its own policy and special requirements for printing announcements. You will need to inquire as to any specifics in addition to deadlines and fees. Check with the life-style editor of each individual newspaper as to their guidelines concerning the following:

1. Will the paper allow you to have either your engagement or your wedding photo published but not both? If you choose the engagement photo, it is customary to have it printed six months to one year prior to the wedding date.

2. What is their policy on submitting and returning photos after they have been printed? Be certain to submit either a 5" x 7" or an 8" x 10" glossy black-and-white photo with your name, address, and telephone number written on a piece of paper and attached to the back of the photo. Your photo should also be protected by being placed in a large envelope with a stiff piece of cardboard.

3. What is their policy on printing your announcement without a photo? If you do wish your announcement printed without a photo, you may do so anytime up to a month before the wedding day.

4. Fill out their form so that it is legible; typing is usually best. Always use full names for all parties included—no initials or nicknames. Make certain to double check all of your information so that it is correct. Include the city where each person named is living with the understanding that every paper will edit this information differently. For the sake of discussion, let us assume that the announcement on page 32 is being run in Washington, D.C., where the bride currently resides. Other cities, such as the home of the groom's parents and the location of the wedding, are mentioned only when the ceremony will not take place in the city where the paper is published. As long as the newspaper editor has all of the information, it can easily be adapted to the appropriate style.

If the paper does not have a printed form, you can type your own, being certain to include a daytime number where you can be reached if there are questions. You will want to be sure to include the following information in any newspaper announcement:

- ♌ Names of you and the groom
- ♌ Schools attended and any degrees received
- ♌ Current places of employment and job titles for both of you
- ♌ Both parents' names
- ♌ The date and location (month and city) of the wedding ceremony and reception (It is unwise to list the family's street address and the day of the wedding.)

5. Make certain that you have some sort of contractual agreement stating how much you are being charged, if anything, and on what date the announcement will appear. With some city newspapers, you are allowed to request the date on which you would like your announcement to be printed. If you do make such a request, remember that Sunday is always the most popular day, which brings its own set of advantages and disadvantages.

Your announcement in its simplest form might read as follows:

Mr. and Mrs. John Thomas Moore announce the engagement of their daughter Elizabeth Anne to Alexander Graham Pope, the son of Mr. and Mrs. Jordan Thomas Pope of Alexandria, Virginia. The wedding will take place during December in Richmond.

Your announcement in a more detailed version might be like this:

Mr. and Mrs. Robert David Stacey of Atwater, Maryland, announce the engagement of their daughter Judy Marie to Mr. Douglas Gordon Murdock, son of Mr. and Mrs. Maxwell Lee Murdock, of Atlanta, Georgia.

Miss Stacey is a graduate of the University of Southern California and the University of Utah School of Law. She is now practicing law in Salt Lake City, Utah. Mr. Murdock was graduated from the University of Colorado, where he was president of Sigma Nu fraternity. He is now attending medical school at the University of Utah. The wedding will take place in June in Salt Lake City.

If your parents are divorced and friendly, they may choose to announce your engagement together:

> Mr. John Val Eccles of Elmhurst, Illinois, and Mrs. Anna Julien Eccles of Los Angeles, California, announce the engagement of their daughter Pamela Ann to David Paul Norris, the son of Mr. and Mrs. David John Norris, of Pocatello, Idaho.

If your parents are divorced and not friendly, both parents are mentioned but the announcement is made by the parent with whom you are living. If your mother is making the announcement, she can have her name listed in the manner she prefers. Most divorced women today are using their given name and their married surname: Mrs. Josephine Smith.

Here is an example of how the announcement might read:

> Mrs. Josephine Smith announces the engagement of her daughter Sarah Vanessa to William Blaine Balken, the son of Mr. and Mrs. Jonathan Blaine Balken of White Plains, New York. Miss Smith is also the daughter of Mr. Michael John Smith of San Francisco, California.

If your mother has remarried and she will be announcing the engagement, she uses her current married surname:

> Mr. and Mrs. Darrell Lawrence Olson announce the engagement of Mrs. Olson's daughter, Connie Louise Schaffer, to Craig Adam Lindell, the son of Mr. and Mrs. James Dale Lindell of Portland, Oregon. Miss Schaffer is also the daughter of Mr. Gary Schaffer of Seattle, Washington. A February wedding is planned in Honolulu, Hawaii.

If one of your parents is deceased, the announcement may read:

> The engagement of Miss Jennifer Ann Lindquist, daughter of Mrs. Jonathan Wayne Lindquist and the late Mr. Lindquist, to Mr. Clayton Thomas Brown, Jr. is announced by the bride's mother. Mr. Brown is the son of Mr. and Mrs. Clayton Thomas Brown, Sr. of Canton, Ohio. The marriage will take place in Canton.

If you and your fiancé are sponsoring the wedding, you may choose to announce the engagement yourselves. It might read as follows:

Linda Christine Hansen, president of I.H.P. International, is to be married to David Glen Browning, president of Oneida Incorporated, in Billings, Montana. Miss Hansen is the daughter of Mr. and Mrs. Gordon Jonathan Hansen of Mesa, Arizona. Mr. Browning is the son of Mrs. Glenda Browning of Miami, Florida, and Mr. Lawrence James Browning of Peoria, Illinois.

Traditionally, your fiancé's parents should never announce the engagement, even if they live a great distance from your family and it appears in their hometown newspaper. Should your fiancé's parents be represented by one of the exceptions listed above, you can adapt the wording to fit his particular set of circumstances.

With all of the remarriages that occur in today's society, it is becoming more and more common for second marriages to be announced in the same manner as a first marriage. It is not necessary to mention the previous marriage and the new engagement announcement can be made by your parents or by you and the groom. If your second marriage follows very closely behind the end of the first marriage, you may wish to announce the wedding only and not the engagement.

Who can enjoy alone?

John Milton

Newspaper Engagement Worksheet

Bride-elect's Last Name _____

Fiancé's Last Name _____

Date to Appear in Paper _____

Bride-elect's Full Name _____

Address _____

City/State _____

Phone (Daytime) _____

Bride-elect Attends/Attended/
Graduated from _____

Bride-elect's Occupation _____

Employed by _____

City/State _____

Bride's Parents' Full Names _____

Address _____

City/State _____

Phone _____

Fiancé's Full Name _____

Fiancé Attends/Attended/
Graduated from _____

Fiancé's Occupation _____

Employed by _____

City/State _____

Fiancé's Parents' Full Names _____

Address _____

City/State _____

Phone _____

Month of Wedding _____

Place of Wedding _____

Will Photo Be Submitted? _____

Other Information _____

_____

_____

_____

_____

40

The Engagement Party

After you have announced your engagement, formally or informally, several parties, showers, and dinners are certain to be given in your honor.

The engagement party, the first of such celebrations, traditionally takes place after you have told immediate family and friends of your engagement and upcoming marriage but before the announcement appears in the newspapers. In very large communities, the announcement may come out in the newspaper before the engagement party or it is becoming more common to have the engagement party the same day the announcement appears in the paper. There is usually six months to one year from the time of the announcement to the day of the wedding.

Betrothals were once marked by a party called a "flouncing," where the couple met with both sets of future in-laws. From that moment on, the engagement was official. The newly engaged bride-to-be could not be seen speaking to another man, nor could her intended talk to another woman. There was no changing your mind after the social event of meeting both families. If the bride-to-be were to call off the engagement after the "flouncing" had taken place, her fiancé would have the right to claim half of her worldly possessions as his own.

Similarly, if he were to change his mind, she would have the same rights to his property.

It has been the custom for many generations to have the engagement party given by your parents. It is becoming more common, however, to have the party hosted by the parents of the groom-to-be or close friends. If you and the groom have been on your own for a while or live in a community a distance from your parents, you may even want to give the party yourselves.

If yours is a non-traditional family, your choices concerning the details of the engagement party—who hosts it, who attends and its formality—should be made in consideration of the feelings of those involved—you, your parents and, perhaps, your stepparents and your fiancé and his family. Just because there is a divorce in either family, these events need not be awkward.

If your mother or your mother and stepfather are hosting the party, you will want to ask your father to attend and for his guest list. If your father is remarried and his wife is not accepted by the family, she may choose not to attend or they may prefer to have a separate party for you and the groom at a later time. The same will apply to your mother if your father hosts the party.

If your parents are divorced and regardless of whether one or both are remarried, your mother and father may choose to host the party together, with the stepparents attending as guests.

If your father has remarried and you are close to both your mother and your stepmother, the three of them may choose to host the party. The same rules apply if your mother has remarried and you are close to your father and stepfather.

If both parents are remarried, both couples may want to host the party together. Do not forget that whoever hosts the party–parents, stepparents, or a combination of both–all names should be included on the invitation.

If you decide to host your own party, you may choose to invite family and friends over for "just a party" and make the very first announcement of your engagement at this time. You may choose to have it announced at the party by your father, who proposes a toast to you, the groom and your future in-laws. Or, if the engagement is a surprise to even the closest family members, you may want to have a large wedding cake in the middle of the buffet table or miniature wedding cakes served individually for dessert as a "subtle" hint as to the reason for the party. It will be a surprise that you and your guests will remember for a long time to come.

If you are one who loves tradition, you will not want to wear your engagement ring until the night of your party or until the announcement has been published in the newspaper. Your engagement ring is usually your fiancé's engagement gift to you. You do not have to give him a gift, but if you choose to do so, the engagement party may be the perfect time to present him with it. It should be something personal and lasting, perhaps a wrist watch that you have had engraved or a leather-bound edition of his favorite book; a gift that is becoming increasingly popular is a groom's engagement ring.

Your engagement party can be a formal affair, a western barbecue, or a wine and cheese party. If the party is very formal, engraved invitations are issued by the host and hostess for the occasion. If engraved invitations are issued, it is practically a promise that a large, formal wedding will follow. If the engagement party is to be less formal, handwritten, purchased invitations or a telephone call are suitable. Invitations to engagement parties may or may not mention the reason for the party. They are generally sent in the name of your parents or of the relative or friend who is announcing the engagement and hosting the party. They are sent to guests who include your family and friends, the wedding party, the groom's parents, even if you realize distance will prevent their attending, and their family and friends. Whether or not to invite step families is something you and the groom should consider carefully. Generally invitations are not sent to guests who will not be invited to the wedding.

Guests are not expected to bring presents but they often do. You and your fiancé will want to wait and open the gifts at another time with just close family and/or friends present.

However large or small your engagement party is, remember you and your fiancé are the guests of honor. This is a very special occasion that officially makes your intentions public, gives all of those close to you the opportunity to offer their congratulations and best wishes, and allows friends and families to become acquainted. Make certain that, as the guests of honor, you and the groom make all of the necessary introductions. You may be the only two who know everyone—either together or individually—so it is up to you to make certain everyone is introduced. Often, it is best to procure everyone's attention at a specific time early in the evening (or at the beginning of the dinner, if a meal is being served), at which time you and the groom individually introduce everyone. You will want to give their name and their association to either or both of you.

At this time, with the guests assembled and their attention procured (or at the dinner table if a sit-down meal is being served), your father proposes a toast to you and your fiancé. Everyone, except you and the groom, raise their glasses and drink. The guests congratulate both of you and then the groom-to-be answers with a toast to you and your family and, perhaps, a short speech. When he is finished, other toasts may follow.

Regardless of who is hosting the party, a guest list complete with addresses and telephone numbers will need to be furnished by you and the groom. The hostess should give you an approximate number of guests to invite, and then you and your fiancé should make out the list, keeping within that number. (Traditionally, all of this was done by your mother but times have changed, as they say.)

Make certain you write a heartfelt thank-you note and, perhaps, even send a small gift of appreciation to the host/hostess of your engagement party. A nice bottle of wine, a bouquet of roses, or an invitation to a special Sunday brunch with you and the groom are always nice ideas.

Engagement Party Checklist

Host/Hostess _____

Address _____

Phone _____

Location of Party _____

Date _____

Time _____

Reservation _____

Theme of Party _____

Menu _____

Cost per Plate _____

Total Cost _____

Invitations Ordered _____

Guest List _____

_____

_____

_____

_____

_____

Thank-You Notes for Engagement Party

Host/Hostess _____

Thank-You Gift _____

Date Thank-You Sent _____

Name _____

Gifts Received _____

_____

_____

_____

_____

Notes:

Wedding Calendar

The next link in the chain of wedding events is for you to sit down and make a calendar, thoroughly listing what needs to be done and when. In addition to going to work or school or both every day, there are so many details to be remembered and attended to and so many tasks that need to be completed–not to mention the good times that you have planned–that doing it all will be impossible if you do not have a calendar for planning ahead and a checklist for what needs to be done and what has been completed.

You will want to buy a calendar that has room to write several notations under each day or you will want to make one of your own, beginning your calendar six months before the day of the wedding.

Six or More Months before the Wedding

♤ Announce your engagement to family and friends as well as in the newspaper.

♤ Have engagement party.

- ♤ Decide on style of wedding.

- ♤ Discuss the financing with your groom and both families.

- ♤ Plan wedding budget.

- ♤ Decide on size of wedding.

- ♤ Prepare guest lists:
    Bride's
    Bride's family
    Groom's
    Groom's family

- ♤ Set wedding date and time.

- ♤ Select and invite all wedding party participants:
    Honor attendant (maid/matron-of honor)
    Bride's attendants
    Best man
    Groomsmen and/or ushers
    Flower girl and ring bearer

- ♤ Consult clergy.

- ♤ Select wedding coordinator.

- ♤ Select wedding location and make reservations.

- Select reception location and make reservations.

- Plan ceremony:
  - Type of ceremony
  - Style of ceremony
  - Ceremony vows
  - Select ceremony participants
  - Decide on music
  - Plan the program
  - Decide on flowers
  - Plan transportation
  - Parking

- Plan reception:
  - Cake
  - Caterer
  - Food
  - Liquor
  - Servers
  - Flowers

- Plan rehearsal and rehearsal dinner.

- Select wedding dress and accessories.

- Select attire and accessories for attendants.

- Select attire and accessories for groomsmen.

- Select attire and accessories for flower girl and ring bearer.

- ☪ Make preliminary reservations for out-of-town guests and wedding participants.

- ☪ Select wedding night suite.

- ☪ Decide on honeymoon:
    - Location
    - Travel reservations
    - Hotel accommodations
    - Transportation

Five Months before the Wedding

- ☪ Decide on decorations for the reception if there are to be any.

- ☪ Select and meet with florist.

- ☪ Select and meet with band/musicians/disc jockey.

- ☪ Select and meet with photographer.

- ☪ Select and meet with videographer.

- ☪ Make final honeymoon plans.

- ☪ Decide on where the two of you will live and begin looking.

- ☪ Meet with stationer and select stationery, enclosures, announcements, and thank-you notes.

Four Months before the Wedding

♪ Select wedding rings.

♪ Finalize ceremony:
>Write and review wedding vows.
>Select special readings and prayers.
>Consult with clergy on ceremony.

♪ Set date and time and make reservations for ceremony rehearsal and rehearsal dinner party.

♪ Register china, silver, crystal, and gifts with selected stores.

Three Months before the Wedding

♪ Check final invitation list.

♪ Have mothers select gowns, consulting with you and each other.

♪ Schedule maid/matron-of-honor (and brides-maids, if necessary) to help address all wedding invitations.

♪ Address and stamp invitation and announce-ment envelopes.

♪ Schedule attendants' dress and shoe fittings.

- ♎ Schedule a physical check-up for you and the groom.

- ♎ Finalize entertainment guide for out-of-town guests.

- ♎ Order wedding accessories, such as ring cushion.

- ♎ Arrange for all rental equipment.

- ♎ Order wedding cake and groom's cake.

- ♎ Make arrangements to have bridal portrait taken.

- ♎ Make final arrangements for transportation.

- ♎ Meet with ceremony and reception musicians and make certain they have all of their music.

Two Months before the Wedding

- ♎ Have final fitting for wedding gown.

- ♎ Set date and make reservations for brides-maids' luncheon.

- ♎ Set date and make reservations for bachelor party.

- Stuff and mail invitations.

- Buy attendants' and groomsmen's gifts.

- Finalize all arrangements in regard to reception.

- Finalize arrangements with caterer.

- Finalize orders for flowers.

- Finalize order for decorations and additional accessories.

- Finalize arrangements for parking and attendants.

- Prepare calendars and checklists for ceremony participants.

- Prepare calendars and checklists for reception participants.

- Prepare wedding reception agenda.

- Buy present for the groom (or the bride).

- Finalize hotel reservations for out-of-town guests and send confirmation letters.

- Arrange transportation for out-of-town guests.

One Month before the Wedding

- ♤ Apply for marriage license.

- ♤ Get blood tests.

- ♤ Have bridal portrait taken.

- ♤ Have florist visit ceremony and reception sites and make all final arrangements.

- ♤ Schedule final fittings for attendants and groomsmen.

- ♤ Mail invitations for rehearsal and rehearsal dinner.

- ♤ Mail invitations for bridesmaids' luncheon.

- ♤ Mail invitations for bachelor dinner.

- ♤ Change insurance policies.

- ♤ Change name and address on driver's license, credit cards and other documents.

- ♤ Write new will and prenuptual agreement.

- ♤ Experiment with wedding hairstyle and make-up.

- ♤ Determine seating arrangements for reception and write place cards.

⚘ Arrange for a place for attendants to dress.

⚘ Prepare, deliver and discuss calendars and checklists for ceremony participants.

⚘ Prepare, deliver and discuss calendars and checklists for reception participants.

⚘ Give photographer checklist of wedding photos and calendar, confirming arrangements.

⚘ Give videographer checklist of events.

⚘ Give caterer final head count and seating chart and confirm all other details.

⚘ Record all gifts and write thank yous as they arrive.

⚘ Finalize transportation arrangements for out-of-town guests.

Two Weeks before the Wedding

⚘ Confirm, review, and coordinate all services one last time:
>   Caterer
>   Flowers
>   Photographer
>   Others

○ Confirm lodging arrangements for out-of-town guests one last time.

○ Have bridesmaids' luncheon.

○ Have bachelor party.

One Week before the Wedding

○ Plan a quiet dinner for you and your fiancé.

○ Pack going-away clothing.

○ Pack for honeymoon.

○ Have rehearsal and rehearsal dinner.

○ Deliver announcements to your mother or maid-of-honor to be mailed the day of the wedding.

The Morning of the Wedding

○ Have your hair done.

○ Make certain that anything that is not being delivered is picked up.

○ You, or someone else, should reconfirm plans with the wedding coordinator, florist, photographer and musicians.

- Check to see that the groom has given the ring to the best man.

- Eat breakfast!

Two Hours before the Wedding

- Have your attendants arrive at the prearranged location to begin dressing and assist with any last-minute details.

One Hour before the Ceremony

- Attendants, parents, groomsmen, and groom should arrive at the ceremony location for pictures or any last-minute details.

Forty-five Minutes before the Ceremony

- The musicians begin playing introductory music.

- Ushers begin escorting guests to their seats.

One Half Hour before the Ceremony

- Church officiant gives any last-minute instructions to the groom and groomsmen and/or ushers.

- ♤ Marriage license is given to church officiant.

- ♤ Fee is given to church officiant by the best man.

- ♤ If the wedding is a formal one, you and your father leave for the ceremony site at this time.

Ten Minutes to Go

- ♤ Wedding party and family go the vestibule and wait.

- ♤ Ushers escort grandmothers of the bride to their seats.

- ♤ Ushers escort grandmothers of the groom to their seats.

- ♤ Other honored guests are escorted to their seats.

- ♤ For a traditional and formal entrance, you and your father arrive at the church and join the wedding party.

Five Minutes to Go

- ♤ The groom's mother is escorted to her seat, preferably by a member of the groom's family, with her husband following closely behind.

- Any last-minute guests are seated.

- Your mother is escorted to her seat.

- The musical solo begins.

One Minute to Go

- Two ushers lay the aisle runner.

Ceremony Time

- The officiant takes his position.

- The groom, accompanied by the best man, enters to the front of the altar.

- The processional music begins.

One Month following the Wedding

- Write and mail thank-you notes.

- Return duplicate wedding gifts.

Wedding Issues

After you have become engaged and formally announced and celebrated it at the engagement party, it is time to begin discussing specific details for your wedding, reception and future together—all very important links in the chain of events.

The Wedding Style

The third link you will want to decide on is the style of your wedding and reception. Choose the style of ceremony and festivities to follow that reflects the feelings, desires, and beliefs of both you and the groom. If that style is a traditional religious ceremony, then the circumstances are dictated by the officiant, but if it is any variation on this theme, the two of you should express your desires and make certain they are incorporated into the entire wedding plan. What follow are some brief descriptions for style and a chart to help give you an overall picture of what each style represents.

Very Formal/Formal

The very formal/formal wedding and reception to follow are steeped in tradition and laced with all of the pageantry and finery the occasion has to offer. The ceremony is eloquent and religious, the wedding party is extensive, the reception is large and lavish with a sit-down dinner or extensive buffet, and every detail is carried to the extreme, making this an occasion that will truly be remembered.

Semiformal

Most formal wedding procedures apply to the somewhat smaller, semiformal wedding ceremony and reception. The ceremony may or may not be of a religious nature and all other details are patterned after the formal affair, just on a smaller scale. The wedding party consists of fewer members and the reception has a nice buffet and dancing. All other details are attended to with careful attention but not carried to "extreme."

Informal

An intimate, informal wedding event may be held anywhere from a small chapel to your home. The ceremony and reception are small and simple, yet lovely and memorable.

Traditional

The traditional wedding is usually religious in nature with the reception that follows containing all of the events you might expect at a wedding: a receiving line, traditional toasts to you and the groom, a cutting of the cake ceremony, the throwing of the bouquet, dancing, and the traditional departure with the throwing of rice.

Nontraditional

The nontraditional wedding and ceremony are for the bride and groom who think taking vows in a church with a reception to follow is entirely too mainstream for their wants or needs. This style of festivities is usually associated with what the bride and groom like to do best. It can range from being married underwater with a clam bake on the beach to a garden wedding at a resort.

Whichever you choose, anything from the most formal to the most contemporary, the choice should be one that you and the groom decide on together, that reflects your life-style, and that will fit nicely into your budget. (For more detailed information on ceremony styles, see *Wedding Ceremonies,* and for more detailed information on reception styles, see *Wedding Receptions*, both by Jo Packham.)
The following charts will help give you an overall picture of what each style represents.

	Very Formal	Formal	Semiformal	Informal
Style	Traditional, expensive, elaborate	More relaxed, most popular	Between formal and informal	Whatever you desire
Invitations/Announcements	Engraved on heavy, white or ivory paper; card folded; two envelopes; enclosures	Engraved or printed on heavy, white or ivory paper; single or folded card– one or two envelopes; enclosures	Printed on any color paper, additions such as photographs one envelope	Printed or handwritten on any color paper or style that is appropriate
Ceremony	Church, synagogue, temple, ballroom, country club	Church, synagogue, temple, ballroom, country club, home	Anywhere that is appropriate	Anywhere desired
Reception	Large, lavish dinner and music	Dinner and music	Usually includes meal, maybe music	Small and simple
Food/Beverages	Champagne, liquor optional Sit-down or buffet, bridal party and guests have tables	Champagne or punch, other drinks optional Buffet, bridal party may have tables	Champagne for toasts, other drinks optional Stand-up buffet	Champagne for toasts, tea, coffee, other drinks optional Snacks or cake

	Very Formal	Formal	Semiformal	Informal
Decorations/Accessories	Elaborate flowers for church and reception. Limousines, canopy, pew ribbons, aisle carpet, groom's cake, engraved napkins	Flowers for church, same accessories as very formal Limousines and other items optional	Flowers for altar, same decorations for reception	Whatever you desire
Music	Organ at church, choir optional, dancing at reception	Organ at church, soloist optional, dancing optional	Organ at church	Usually no music
Guest List	Over 200 guests	75–200 guests	Under 100 guests	Not more than 50 guests
Bride	Elegant, long dress, long sleeves/ gloves, long train, veil	Long dress, any sleeve length, veil, shorter train	Morning wedding-knee length Evening-floor length, veil/hat/ wreath	Dress or suit with hat, or casual, if appropriate
Males	Cutaway, long jacket or stroller for day; tailcoat for night	Cutaway, stroller or tuxedo for day; tuxedo for night	Stroller, tuxedo, dinner jacket for day; tuxedo, dinner jacket, suit or blazer for evening	Business suit, blazer
Females	6–8 attendants Elegant, long dress, long sleeves/ gloves	2–6 attendants Long dress, any sleeve length	1–3 attendants Morning wedding-knee length Evening-floor length	1 attendant Dress or suit or casual if appropriate

Finances

Next, you and the groom will want to discuss the finances for the wedding festivities. It is of the utmost importance that the two of you discuss this subject openly and honestly. Your wedding is a celebration that you want to share with family and friends and that you want to remember as one of the happiest times of your life and theirs as well. If the events become a financial strain on the budget of either you, the groom, or one of your families, it will be remembered for exactly that. Remember that it is not the amount of money that is spent that will make your wedding memorable, but it is the creativity and the careful planning that will make it the affair you always dreamed of.

Traditionally, you and your family pay for most of the wedding and reception costs. Today, however, with long-distance weddings, divorced parents, second marriages, and uneven guest lists, many rules and roles have changed. You may want to read the following guidelines and then adapt them to your own specific needs. What is most important is that you talk openly with everyone involved and be sensitive to their willingness and ability to be involved financially.

Expenses for You and/or Your Family

1. The engagement party, if they host it

2. The invitations, announcements, enclosure cards, personal stationery, and thank-you notes, including stamps for mailing

3. Your wedding dress, veil, and accessories

4. Your trousseau of clothes and lingerie

5. Their own wedding attire and the attire required for any family members still living at home

6. The groom's ring

7. A wedding gift for you and the groom

8. Gifts for your attendants

9. All hotel accommodations for your out-of-town attendants

10. Any bridal consultant fees

11. All expenses of the ceremony, except for those specified as the groom's family expenses (see page 70), including rental fee for the church or ceremony site and fees for any additional equipment such as aisle carpets or candle holders

12. Fees for all wedding participants (other than family members, friends, or relatives), such as the organist, soloist, or band members, but not including the ceremony official

13. All expense of the reception
- **a.** Rental fee for the reception site
- **b.** All food and beverage charges
- **c.** All catering charges
- **d.** The wedding cake or cakes
- **e.** Music for the reception
- **f.** Fees for such items as guest book or wedding gift register
- **g.** Fees for additional equipment
- **h.** Fees for additional help

14. The following flowers:
- **a.** All flowers used for decorating the ceremony and reception sites
- **b.** Bouquets or corsages for the brides-maids, honor attendants and the flower girl
- **c.** Flowers or corsages for any other wedding participants in addition to the wedding party
- **d.** Corsages or flowers given to any special relatives or friends who may have helped
- **e.** Flowers sent to any hostess who entertained for you or for you and the groom before your wedding day

15. Your photograph taken before the ceremony

16. All photography and any recordings or videotaping of the ceremony or reception

17. All charges for transporting the bridal party to the church and from the church to the reception site

18. All expenses involved in parking cars, security, and traffic control

Expenses for the Groom and/or His Family

1. Your engagement and wedding rings

2. A wedding gift for you and the groom

3. The marriage license

4. Their personal wedding attire and accessories

5. Gloves, ties, and ascots for all men in the wedding party

6. Hotel accommodations for the groom's out-of-town groomsmen

7. Gifts for the best man and out-of-town groomsmen

8. The rehearsal dinner

9. Ceremony official's fee

10. Your flowers, including going-away corsages and throwing bouquet

11. Groom's boutonniere and those for his groomsmen

12. Corsages for mothers and grandmothers

13. Complete honeymoon trip

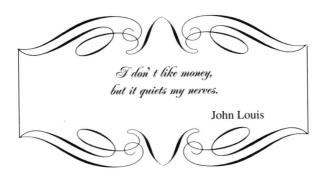

I don't like money, but it quiets my nerves.

John Louis

Budgets

After determining between the two of you who will finance the wedding, you need to establish a budget for your wedding. This will require setting priorities. First, the two of you must decide what it is that you care about the most. Is it the food, the flowers, your dress? Then you need to carefully prepare your budget and promise yourselves to adhere to that budget. It is so easy to add $100 here and $100 there and pretty soon you have doubled the amount you had first estimated.

Begin your budgeting process by taking the monies that are available and devising a budget by category that will set the limits of how much can be spent on individual items such as your dress, the cake and the invitations.

Adapt the following checklists to meet your needs, making certain you use them whenever you are meeting with someone who is providing goods or services for the wedding or the reception. Because this is a general, overall checklist to note total expenditures in each category, you will want to have complete and detailed checklists for each category to work from.

Ceremony Expenses

	Estimated Costs	Actual Costs	Who Pays
Your Attire Dress			
Shoes			
Accessories			
Groom's Attire Tuxedo or suit			
Shoes			
Accessories			
Invitations			
Enclosures Ceremony Cards			
Reception Cards			
Pew Cards			
Admission Cards			
Rain Cards			
Travel Cards			
Maps			
Long-Weekend Cards			
At-Home Cards			
Response Cards			

	Estimated Costs	Actual Costs	Who Pays
Thank-You Notes			
Announcements			
Gift for Honor Attendant			
Gift for Best Man			
Gifts for Bridesmaids			
Gifts for Groomsmen			
Site Fees			
Participants Ceremony Officiant			
Musical Participant(s)			
Soloist(s)			
Flowers			
Additional Decorations			
Aisle Carpets			
Candle Holders			
Additional Equipment			
Transportation			
Parking Attendants			
Facility Fees			
Rehearsal Dinner Site			
Cost per Plate			

Reception Expenses

	Estimated Costs	Actual Costs	Who Pays
Site Fees			
Caterer/Food			
Waiters			
Liquor/Bar			
Bar Tender			
Additional Equipment			
Wedding Cakes			
Accessories			
Cake Knife			
Toasting Glasses			
Guest Book			
Rice Bags			
Other			

	Estimated Costs	Actual Costs	Who Pays
Reception Flowers			
Buffet Table Flowers			
Table Centerpieces			
Cake Table			
Guest Book Table			
Rice/Potpourri Bags			
Other Decorations			
Photography			
Videography			
Music			
Transportation			
Parking Attendants			
Facility Fees			
Security			
Other			

The Site

You will want to begin your search for ceremony and reception sites as soon as possible. Prime dates can booked up to a year in advance. If you are planning to have the ceremony in your church, then the site selection is easy. If you are undecided as to where to hold the ceremony, you will want to contact outside resources to help you with your search. Possibilities for ceremony location sites are a church, temple, synagogue, or rectory; a hotel, club, or restaurant; a city hall or the office of a justice of the peace; a wedding chapel; at home; outdoors (either at a home or in a public place such as a park or historical site); or a myriad of contemporary options such as on a private rail car, aboard ship, or at a local resort. (For very detailed information on site selection for ceremonies, refer to *Wedding Ceremonies* by Jo Packham.)

Once the site for the ceremony is determined, you can choose to have the reception at the same location or elsewhere. In making your choice, consider the time of day, your religious beliefs, the availability of the site and the formality of the occasion. The time of your reception determines, to a certain extent, what type it will be. (These matters are discussed in detail in *Wedding Receptions* by Jo Packham.)

Your Attendants

Next you will need to select your attendants and groomsmen.

Asking someone to be a wedding participant is not only an ancient custom but an honor and a great responsibility. In the past, there were definite rules about whom would be included and absolute guidelines on what their roles should be, and every member of the wedding party had a well-defined area of responsibility. Today, however, with modern mobility, career obligations, and scattered families, you and your fiancé will have to decide what is best for the two of you, your families, and your wedding participants. You may want to begin with the traditional guidelines and then rewrite them to suit your own personal wants and needs.

You will both want to include family and friends in your wedding party. Contact all wedding party members and ask them to participate immediately after the engagement is announced and contact all of them as close to the same time as possible. The invitation to participate should be delivered in person unless that is impossible due to distance.

Remember that not everyone may be aware of all of his or her responsibilities as a member of the wedding party. Do not assume that they know what is expected of them and do not hesitate to talk to them about their duties, responsibilities, and your expectations. Never expect more of your wedding party than they can reasonably afford to give–both in time and financial considerations. You want your wedding to be as memorable for your participants as you do for you and the groom. (For detailed information on selecting your wedding party, see *Wedding Attendants* by Jo Packham.)

The Guest List

Next you will need to decide who is going to be invited to the wedding, the reception or both. As a general rule, 75 percent of those invited will actually attend if your wedding is on a weekend, 60 percent if it is during the week. There are several considerations when arriving at a number for your guest list: your budget; your wedding style; and your, the groom's, and both family's wishes on how many to include. You will want to sit down with both families and discuss the number that you can accommodate and afford to invite, as well as details such as your policy on inviting children. Now is the time to determine how to divide the guest list, making a provision for how to also divide expenses should one party invite a larger number of guests than the other.

Now you can begin coordinating the details for the wedding and reception. With careful planning, you can be assured of the "perfect" wedding event. Remember to include the groom in any major decisions concerning the wedding festivities. Getting his advice will not only help but will get your marriage off on a positive note of communicating and sharing.

Set the date, select a time, and attend to each and every detail individually. Due to your state of mind as a bride-to-be and the number of details to be attended to, you will want to have complete itemized checklists for every aspect of the wedding and reception. This will be an impossible and overwhelming task if you are not organized and do not keep thorough and accurate records.

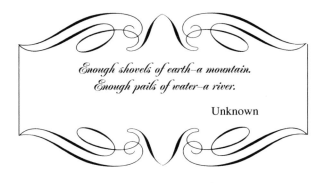

Enough shovels of earth–a mountain.
Enough pails of water–a river.

Unknown

Canceling the Engagement

In today's fast-paced, unpredictable world, we all make decisions that we come to realize are not in our best interest. In any situation such as this, it is much easier to cancel your plans in midstream than to continue with them and hope that everything will work out the way you had dreamed it would. You must be very careful in either situation and not act too hastily. This one event will probably change your life more than any other, so it is natural to be doubtful, apprehensive, or confused, or to have mixed feelings.

If you look at the situation carefully and decide that the marriage should not take place, you may want to start by simply postponing it for a period of time that you feel is adequate to work out the problems. If your decision is to cancel the wedding plans altogether, do not be embarrassed by your decision to do so. Everyone makes mistakes and you do not need to spend the rest of your life paying for them because you are embarrassed to handle them now. Begin by making a personal visit to your parents and explain to them your decision and the reason for the decision. You may then choose to visit the groom's parents or to write them a short note explaining the situation, being careful not to place the blame on either party. You then will want to write a short note to other family members and close friends.

If, for any reason, you and the groom choose to postpone the wedding and another date has been set, guests may be notified by a new printed invitation, if there is time, patterned in the same style as the original. If there is not time for a printed declaration, guests may be sent a handwritten note, signed by the person who issued the invitations. Guests may also be called or sent a telegram in the name of the person(s) who issued the invitations. No reason needs to be given for the postponement.

If the engagement is broken after the invitations have been mailed and if there is adequate time before the day of the ceremony, engraved or printed notices are sent, recalling the wedding invitation. Again, the announcement is in the same style as the invitation and is issued by the person(s) who sent the invitations. If the engagement is broken too close to the day of the wedding for printed notices to be prepared, the invited guests are notified by telephone or telegram with the messages being made in the name of the person(s) who issued the invitations. No reason need be given for the broken engagement.

Topics for Discussion During Your Engagement

In addition to making plans for and discussing the details of the wedding ceremony and reception, several other topics will need to be discussed and issues agreed upon before the wedding actually takes place. Most of these topics are pragmatic matters and fairly delicate, the kind which two people in love might choose not to discuss because they are so busy with all of the wedding plans and they are certain that "their love will find the answers." Well, the plans that are taking so much time are for an event that will last for only one day and your marriage should last a lifetime. It is, therefore, important that you find time to talk about these and related issues. If discussed in the beginning, openly and honestly, it will set a tone for a marriage that is itself open and honest, one of sharing and understanding.

Changing Names

One such topic that is a very contemporary issue is what name will you, the bride, choose to use? As a woman, the choice is yours, but it should be discussed with your fiancé. Will you retain your maiden name, hyphenate both names, or take his last name? You can base your decision on several considerations: first, the feelings the two of you have toward this particular issue; second, the ease of pronunciations and spelling; third, your professional status; fourth, a wish to carry on your family name, or, fifth, your desire to handle manners in a traditional way.

♌ Many women choose to use their maiden name as their middle name. If you choose to do so, you sign everything "Judy Pledger Macfarlane" rather than "Judy Marie Macfarlane."

♌ If you plan to keep your maiden name, you are not required to offer any official notification. In most instances, you simply continue to sign legal documents the way you always have. In some cases, such as buying property, applying for credit cards as husband and wife, or if you are involved in other legal transactions or issues, because you and your husband each have a different last name, you may have to offer proof that you are indeed married.

♧ If you hyphenate your surname and your husband's, you may do so yourself or both you and your husband may decide to hyphen ate. This then becomes "Judy Marie Pledger-Macfarlane" and "John Michael Pledger-Macfarlane." If your choice is to hyphenate, then you will have to take the same steps as you would if you were completely changing your name. Some disadvantages to this choice are, first, your husband may not wish to change his name, so you both continue to have different names, and, second, if both names are long, this can become cumbersome in day-to-day life.

♧ If you hyphenate or change your name, you will want to make certain that you do so on all legal documents and official records. You will need to sign the marriage license with your new name and then you will want to make the change on the documents listed below. Some of these may require a visit to the local office of a given agency as well as presenting your marriage certificate as proof of your marriage.

> Bills for home services (i.e., telephone, electricity and others)
> Checking and savings accounts
> Driver's license
> Employee ID
> Insurance
> Magazine subscriptions

Passport
Social security card
Stocks and bond certificates
Telephone directory
Voter registration
Will

- ♤ In almost all instances, it is important to be
consistent and to let everyone know what you
have decided to do as quickly as possible.
You may want to do the following to help
inform others of your decision:

- ♤ Send at-home cards with your wedding
invitations, announcements, and all thank-
you notes, showing your new name and
address.

- ♤ Use the name you have selected on personal
stationery, letterhead and business cards, and
in all correspondence. Write it out completely
on return addresses (or have it printed in full
on return-address labels) and when signing
anything except very personal correspondence.

- ♤ For business purposes, you may elect to send
announcement cards that state you have
recently married and are either changing your
name to such-and-such or have elected to
keep your maiden name.

- ♤ Indicate in the newspaper wedding announcement that you will be keeping your own name.

- ♤ If you elect to keep your own name, introduce yourself or be introduced at all gatherings using your last name, indicating that you are John MacFarlane's wife.

- ♤ Respond to misaddressed correspondence or invitations with the correct name: Judy Pledger and John MacFarlane will . . .

Do not be offended when the wrong name is used. This may be very confusing to some and it will take a while for everyone to remember exactly what name it is you are using.

In addition to changing your name, there are many other important issues. Counselors agree that among the major problems in a new marriage are the unfulfilled expectations and inconsistent goals. Everyone has certain expectations of what marriage will be like, what a *husband* is supposed to say and do, and what a *wife* is supposed to say and do. And even though you are the same two people who have dated or lived together long enough to think you know and understand one another, the minute you say "I do," some expectations change. When these expectations are not fulfilled, there is bound to be frustration, disappointment and resentment. Remembering that people seldom change, it is, therefore, in your best interest to verbally–and sometimes in writing–express in great detail all of your expectations and plans for the future. Now, during your engagement, is opportune timing. If you cannot agree now, it is unlikely that you will be able to agree later.

The following areas are those that are most often misunderstood and can cause problems:

Career

Will you both work? Full-time or part-time? If you both work, how will you share the responsibilities for running and caring for a house? Is one of your careers more important than the other's? If one party is transferred to another city, will the other agree to go or will a new job have to be found? How many hours do you both consider reasonable to work a day? –a week? Is it acceptable for one or both parties to travel with his/her job? If so, how much? Which comes first, career obligations or family obligations? What exactly are your career goals? Do you want to work until later in life or do you picture yourself retiring early and traveling or living in a small house on the beach?

Children

Do you both want children? If so, immediately or several years from now? Have you discussed an effective and acceptable means of birth control? How many children do you picture yourself raising? If and when you have children, who will take care of them? Will you both continue to work and hire someone, will one of you quit, will you both work part time? If you cannot have children, would you consider adopting?

Family

If both families live in the same town, how do you split up the holidays? How much time is appropriate to spend with each family? Do you ask your families to go places or do you ask friends? How often can you ask your family over or go to their home?

Friends

Do you like each other's friends? Do you like spending a lot of time with friends or do you prefer to be alone together? Is it appropriate to have friends of the opposite sex? How often is it acceptable to "go out" with your friends without your partner? Does it matter where you and your friends go and what you do? What kinds of activities do you enjoy doing with your friends?

Insurance

Make certain that you are both covered by health insurance and that you have insurance on your automobiles. If you have previously been included on your parents' policies, you will need to shop for the best plans with the best companies. Insurance can be confusing and intimidating, but it is very important and needs to be taken care of immediately. This may be one of the first times you really feel grown-up, yet you wish you could just ask your father to take care of it!

Legal Issues

Will there be a prenuptual agreement? How will your wills be changed? Who will become the beneficiary on each other's insurance policies? Who do you select for legal counsel? Will you have a safe deposit box and whose names will be listed on it? Whose names will be listed on the stocks and bonds?

Leisure Time

Will you spend the majority of your free time together or will it be spent apart? What do you enjoy doing in your spare time? Will you both be willing to participate in the other's favorite activities, even if one is obsessed with softball and the other loves the symphony? What kinds of vacations do you both enjoy taking—a more important question than you might realize! Is it appropriate to take separate vacations? How many vacations do you take a year? Do you take three or four long-weekend vacations or one long, two-week trip?

Money

Will you pool your income into one fund and a joint checking account? Will you divide the bills and maintain separate checking accounts? Should you each know what the other makes and how he or she is spending the money? Do you have a budget? Who decides how much is spent where? How much do you allocate for savings each month? Is there a problem with egos if one party makes more than the other? Who decides how the money is to be spent if there is a disagreement?

Religion

Are you both of the same faith? Does it matter if you are not? Will you attend church or temple regularly? If so, which one? Will you attend alone or together? In which faith will your children be raised and what will be expected of them?

Sex

Are you open and honest about your sexual likes and dislikes? If problems develop, how will you handle the situation? Are you agreeable to obtaining outside help?

It is often extremely difficult to sit down and just begin talking about the major issues previously discussed. If one of you says, "Tonight we have to discuss our future" or "Tonight it is important to discuss how we both feel on the issues of career and children," you may both be uneasy and on the defensive. It is a much better idea to take one night a week and go for a long walk, or have a nice, quiet dinner and go window shopping afterwards, or plan an evening at home in front of the fire. These quiet times together naturally lead themselves to long talks, possibly about intimate issues.

In the setting you choose, here is a suggestion for a game of sorts to help you clarify some of what you want and need to know about the other. The game might consist of taking turns and asking each other a series of questions such as these:

How well do you know me?
Where was I born?
What is my nickname and why?
What is my favorite color?
What is my favorite food?
What is my favorite sport?
What do I love to do the most in my spare time?
Where would I most like to go on vacation?
What is my dream car?
If I had a million dollars, how would I spend it?
What five things do I like most about you? About myself?
What five things do I like least about you? About myself?

The list could include questions from several categories and could go on forever until you have asked everything! If you plan a time that is relaxing and involves only the two of you without outside distractions, you will naturally begin talking about the things that are on your mind and you will learn most of the things you need to know.

You both need to understand that a successful marriage involves more hard work than any job you will ever undertake, excellent channels of communication, unlimited support for each other, compatible goals, unquestioning trust, complete honesty, and the ability to compromise and feel good about it.

The ultimate dream of every engaged couple is to live happily ever after–and to do that, you will need to start today and work toward that goal every minute of every day. It will be, however, the most rewarding, the most fun, and the most exciting job you have ever undertaken!

. . . there is no joy
above the joy of the
heart.

Proverb

Index

Come live with me, and be my love,
And we will some new pleasures prove.
Of golden sands, and crystal brooks,
With silken lines, and silver hooks.

John Donne